My Private Property

My Private Property

Mary Ruefle

WAVE BOOKS

SEATTLE AND NEW YORK

PUBLISHED BY WAVE BOOKS

WWW.WAVEPOETRY.COM

COPYRIGHT © 2016 BY MARY RUEFLE

ALL RIGHTS RESERVED

WAVE BOOKS TITLES ARE DISTRIBUTED TO THE TRADE BY

CONSORTIUM BOOK SALES AND DISTRIBUTION

PHONE: 800-283-3572 / SAN 631-760X

LIBRARY OF CONGRESS CATALOGING-IN-PUBLICATION DATA

NAMES: RUEFLE, MARY, 1952– AUTHOR.

TITLE: MY PRIVATE PROPERTY / MARY RUEFLE.

DESCRIPTION: FIRST EDITION. | SEATTLE : WAVE BOOKS, [2016]

IDENTIFIERS: LCCN 2015045705 |

ISBN 9781940696386 (HARDCOVER)

CLASSIFICATION: LCC PS3568.U36 A6 2016 | DDC 811/.54—DC23

LC RECORD AVAILABLE AT HTTP://LCCN.LOC.GOV/2015045705

FIRST PAPERBACK EDITION, 2017

PAPERBACK ISBN 978-1-940696-51-5

DESIGNED AND COMPOSED BY QUEMADURA

PRINTED IN THE UNITED STATES OF AMERICA

9 8 7 6 5 4 3 2

WAVE BOOKS 061

FOR MICHAEL

CONTENTS

The cumbersome bones, the curious distance from foot and fingertip to brain, too; and those quarts and quarts of blood. I shuddered. It was little short of a miracle that they escaped continual injury; and what an extended body in which to die.

WALTER DE LA MARE, *Memoirs of a Midget*

My Private Property

LITTLE GOLF PENCIL

At headquarters they asked me for something dry and understated. Mary, they said, it's called a *statement*. They took me out back to a courtyard where they always ate lunch and showed me a little tree that was, sadly, dying. Something with four legs had eaten it rather badly. Don't over-emote, they said. I promised I wouldn't but I was thinking to myself that the something-with-four-legs had certainly over-emoted and that the tree, in response, was over-emoting now, being in the strange little position of dying. All the cops were sitting around eating sandwich halves and offered me one. This one's delicious, said a lieutenant, my wife made it. Seeing as it was peanut butter and jelly I thought he was over-emoting, but I didn't say anything. I just sat looking at the tree and eating my sandwich half. When I was ready I asked for a pencil and they gave me one of those little golf pencils. I didn't say anything about that, either. I just wrote my statement and handed it over—it was a description of the tree which they intended to give to their captain as a Christmas present—I mean my description, not the tree—because the captain, well, he loved that tree and he loved my writing and every one of the cops hoped to be promoted in the captain's heart and, who knows, maybe get a raise. Still, after all that sitting around in the courtyard eating sandwich halves, I had a nice feeling of sharing, so when they asked me whether I had anything else to say I told them that in the beginning you understand the world but not yourself, and when you finally understand yourself you no longer understand the world. They seemed satisfied with that. Cops, they're all so young.

KEYS

Poor little keys! Success is not always to be expected, for passive resistance having become the creed of keys, it takes the form of what their tormentors call obstinacy, and when it has become hereditary, I am afraid all the world won't get it out of them. All that can be done is to rescue a solitary individual now and then, and try what care and kindness may make of him. Not long ago, shocked at the cruelty with which they were treated, a benevolent gentleman, who had his theories about keys, determined that he would bring up a young key as one raises a young child. A little one was brought, and kept in a hole, but when the time came the key would not come out of his hole, and nothing would ever make him. The key's feelings were those of a snail being pulled from his shell. What became of that key was never known, but it seems certain one hole led to another, and it is my deepest hope that the benevolent gentleman let him live by trying him in ever other holes, and that eventually there passed between them an authentic feeling, even if it was one of defeat.

PLEASE READ

I am the yellow finch that came to her feeder an hour before she died. I was the last living thing she saw, so my responsibility was great. Yet all I did was eat. Through eight long months of winter the black oiled sunflower seeds had gone untouched—not a single one of my kind or any other kind had approached them. It was too much work. Even if we'd had the strength—which we did not, half-starved as we were—we were not in the mood to crack anything. On the morning of the twenty-second of April she took them away and refilled the feeding tube with sunflower hearts—sheeny niblets whose hard outer husk had been stripped away by some faraway, intricate machine. She went back inside and waited. From my branch I could see her do the things she liked to do—she picked up a towel from off the floor, she filled out a card stopping the mail, she boiled water, she stared into space. She saw me coming. Her face flickered with, if not exactly joy, the ordinary wellspring of life. It's true there was a sheet of glass between us. But I could see the seeds of her eyes and the upturned corners of her mouth. I ate a heart. I turned my head. She looked at me as if I were the last living thing on earth. And as I was, I kept on eating.

LUCKY

While I was sleeping God broke into my heart and nailed up pictures of Himself in different clothes. He asked me which one I liked the best, but it was apparent I was to like them all. I didn't like any of them, but there was one, a white robe with a floating blue halo above the neckline where His face should be, and I thought to that picture I could at least express my Fear. So I said I liked it. Immediately He said that I had no taste. I thought I would wake then and there, with a bad taste in my mouth, and choose for the day brightly colored clothes of the kind I would never wear, but that didn't happen. I slept dreamless as a baby, and when I awoke I was naked as a baby, and alone, and afraid.

OBSERVATIONS
ON THE GROUND

The planet seen from extremely close up is called the *ground*. The ground can be made loose by the human hand, or by using a small tool held in the human hand, such as a *spade*, or an even larger tool, such as a *shovel*, or a variety of machines commonly called *heavy equipment*. We bury our dead in the ground. Roughly half the dead are buried in boxes and half the dead are buried without boxes. A burying box is an emblem of respect for the dead. We are the only species to so envelop our dead. An earlier, more minimal, way to envelop the dead was to wrap them in cloth.

Besides burying the dead in the ground, we bury our garbage, also called *trash*. Man-made mountains of garbage are pushed together using heavy equipment and then pushed down into the ground. The site of this burial is called a *landfill*. The site of the dead buried in boxes is called a *cemetery*. In both cases the ground is being filled.

A dead body in a box can be lowered into the ground using heavy equipment, but we do not consider it trash. When the dead are not in boxes and there is a man-made mountain of them we use heavy equipment to bury them together, like trash. It is estimated that everywhere we walk we are walking on a piece of trash and the hard, insoluble remains of the dead. Whatever the case, the dead and the garbage are together in the ground where we cannot see them, for we do not relish the sight or smell of them. If we did not go about our burying, we would be in danger of being overcome.

Also buried in the ground are *seeds*, which we want to see when they emerge from the ground in their later form — that is, as *plants*. Plants rising from the ground are essential to life. To bury a seed is to *plant* it. When a seed is planted and not seen again, those who buried it are made sad. The anticipated plant of the wished-upon seed has not materialized. It is dead, and remains buried. Heavy equipment is used to plant large expanses of ground with seed. When a whole field of shivering grain rises from the earth, there is a growing sense of happiness among those who buried the seeds. Happiness is also present when a tree emerges, or a tree that will bear fruit, or leafy green, edible plants that were formerly planted. When *flowers* arise from the ground, colorful and shapely in an astonishing variety of ways, the living are made *especially* happy. Not only are flowers admired for their outward beauty of form, their scents are capable of overcoming us and therefore prized. Nothing, it seems, makes the living as happy as a flower. Flowers are among the most anticipated things on earth. For this reason, we separate the flower from the ground and present it to another to hold or to look at. After a while, the flower that has been separated from the ground *dies*, and we throw it in the trash. Flowers are often planted where the dead are buried in boxes, but these flowers are *never* cut. That would be *horrible*. Whoever did such a thing would be considered a *thief*. *Those* flowers belong to the dead.

Blue sadness is sweetness cut into strips with scissors and then into little pieces by a knife, it is the sadness of reverie and nostalgia: it may be, for example, the memory of a happiness that is now only a memory, it has receded into a niche that cannot be dusted for it is beyond your reach; distinct and dusty, blue sadness lies in your inability to dust it, it is as unreachable as the sky, it is a fact reflecting the sadness of all facts. Blue sadness is that which you wish to forget, but cannot, as when on a bus one suddenly pictures with absolute clarity a ball of dust in a closet, such an odd, unshareable thought that one blushes, a deep rose spreading over the blue fact of sadness, creating a situation that can only be compared to a temple, which exists, but to visit it one would have to travel two thousand miles on snowshoes and by dogsled, five hundred by horseback and another five hundred by boat, with a thousand by rail.

THE WOMAN WHO COULDN'T DESCRIBE A THING IF SHE COULD

We have a house. There is a roof and there are windows. I think they are square. You can see through them, that's for sure. There is a door to go into and out of the house. It works both ways. And oh, a floor.

We left the house in a car. The car had wheels, there were four of them. And there was a door for going into and out of the car. Actually there were four doors, there were four of us, too, so we each had our own door. Inside there was only room to sit down, and a strap that went across your body in case there was an accident.

An accident is when something happens that is not supposed to happen and you don't want it to but it does anyway. We did not have an accident that day. We went to a restaurant instead.

The car stayed outside the restaurant and we stayed inside the restaurant. A restaurant is a place that will cook for you. You give them money for the cooking. Or for the eating, I am unsure which.

You probably already know this, but eating is when the food goes inside your body. Later it comes out a different door in another way. (When I said the car had four doors I forgot number five, the little door where the gas goes in.)

So we four were in the restaurant. Some of the food was good and some of the food was bad, but it costs the same. As you eat you have a conversation. A conversation is talking between people. One person said "I am tired of the heat," and another said "Me too." I said "I kind of like it." The last of us said "Could we talk about something other than the weather?" I thought that was an interesting thing to say.

A thought is silent talking to yourself in your head. But you can still hear it. This is the number-one difference.

After the eating and the conversation, one of us gave money for these things. You just hand it over and for a moment you can see it, it is moving from one hand to another hand and you can see it, it is paper. But it is not usually shown, most of the time you keep your money out of sight. It is hardly ever in the air. It is not like a necklace or something. But at such and such a time you take it out and give some of it away. You never give your necklace away. All the same a necklace is a sign of money. It just is. You show the sign that you have things hidden. It goes back and forth, like a conversation.

Two of us were wearing necklaces and two of us were not. That is a fact I added together later, so you would know.

We left the restaurant by the door. There was the car. In the car we did not have a conversation. We left the car when it was looking at the house.

Inside the house there was an accident. Accidents happen so fast you never really see them, so no one can really talk about them. After the accident there was another conversation. It was longer than the conversation we had in the restaurant, even though there were four of us in the restaurant and now there were only three.

Then it was time for bed. A bed is where you sleep. If you have a necklace you take it off. Both you and the necklace change from an upright position to a downright position. But not together.

You close your eyes, which have been open all day. You close your mouth, which has been open all day. You think about the day. You have the whole day all to yourself. Then you begin to see things inside your head which you did not put there. It is very dark outside your head and you cannot see much there, but you can see the "put" things inside your head. When that happens, you know you are asleep. You might not know it, but you are.

You are asleep. The day is done. You can't describe it anymore. That's life. It's over.

April's Cryalog

M C x 3
T NC
W C x 3
Th C x 3
Fri C x 1
Sat C x 2
Sun C x 2
Mon C x 3
Thes C x 3
Wed C x 2
Thurs NC
Fri C x 1
Sat C x 1
Sun NC
Mon C x 1
Thes C x 2
Wed C x 2
Thurs C x 1
Fri C x 1 very bad
Sat C x 4 very bad
Sun C x 1
M C x 1
T C x 1
W C x 1 a little
Th NC
Fri C x 1 ↑ 16 "?"
Sat C x 1 "my mommy I think"
Sun NC
M NC
T CCCCC
W C pm
Th C am
Fri C
Sat C

Sun NC
Mon CCC
Thes CCC
Wed CCCC
Fri CCCC
Sat CCC
Sun CC
M CC
T CC
W CC
Th CC
Fri CC
Sat CCCC
Sun CCCC
Mon CCC
T CCC
W CCC
Th . CCC
Fri CCC
Sat CCC
Sun CCC
M CCC
T CCC
W CCC

April has 58 days,
after which it
can't go on.

and so on.

PAUSE

I recently came across an old cryalog that I kept during the month of April in 1998. "C" stands for the fact *I cried*, the number of Cs represents the number of times I cried, and "NC" indicates that I did not cry on that day.

The saddest thing is, I now find the cryalog very funny, and laugh when I look at it.

But when I kept it, I wanted to die. Literally, to kill myself—with an iron, a steaming-hot turned-on iron.

This was not depression, this was menopause.

Reading this, or any other thing ever written about menopause, will not help you in any way, for how you respond to menopause is not up to you, it is up to your body, and though you believe now that you can control your body (such is your strength after all that yoga) you cannot.

Of course, you may be lucky: I know a woman who experienced menopause in no way whatsoever except that one day she realized it had been a couple of years since her last period, which was indeed her *last*.

You hear a lot about hot flashes, but hot flashes are the *least* of it, totally inconsequential in every way: you get as hot as a steam iron at odd moments — so what? The media would have you believe that hot flashes are the single most significant symptom toward which you should direct your attention and *their* products, but when I think of menopause I don't think of hot flashes; I am not here to talk about hot flashes.

Except to tell you that they do not cease even after you have completely gone through menopause; they become a part of your life the way your periods were, they are periodic and, after a while, you stop talking about them.

No, I am here to tell you that one woman, a woman who is the most undepressed, optimistic, upbeat person I know, awoke one morning and walked straight into her kitchen and grabbed a butcher's knife (she is a world-class cook) with the intent of driving it through her heart. That was menopause.

If you take the time to peruse the annals of any nine-teenth-century asylum, as I have, you will discover that the "cause of admittance" for all women over forty is listed as *cessation of menses*. Sometimes I saw the words *change of life*, which sounds like a euphemism *but isn't*.

In other words, you go crazy. When you go crazy, you don't have the slightest inclination to read anything Foucault ever wrote about culture and madness.

It may be that you recall your thirteenth year on earth. Menopause is adolescence all over again, only you are an adult and have to go out into the world every day in ways you did not have to when you were in school, where you were surrounded by other adolescents, safe, or relatively so, in the asylum of junior high.

You are a thirteen-year-old with the experience and daily life of a forty-five-year-old.

You have on some days the desire to fuck a tree, or a dog, whichever is closest.

You have the desire to leave your husband or lover or part-
ner, whatever.

No matter how stable or loving the arrangement, you
want out.

You may decide to take up an insane and hopeless cause.
You may decide to walk to Canada, or that it is high time
you begin to collect old blue china, three thousand pieces
of which will leave you bankrupt. Suddenly the solution
to all problems lies in selling your grandmother's gold
watch or drinking your body weight in cider vinegar. A
kind of wild forest blood runs in your veins.

This, and other behaviors, will horrify you. You will seek
medical help because you are intelligent, and none of the
help will help.

You will feel as if your life is over and you will be ab-
solutely right about that, it is over.

No matter how attractive or unattractive you are, you have
been used to having others look you over when you stood

at the bus stop or at the chemist's to buy tampons. They have looked you over to assess how attractive or unattractive you are, so no matter what the case, you were looked at. Those days are over; now others look straight through you, you are completely *invisible* to them, you have become a *ghost*.

You no longer exist.

Because you no longer exist, you will do anything for attention. You may shave your head or dye your hair or wear striped stockings or scream at complete strangers. You've seen them, haven't you, the middle-aged women screaming at the attendant in the convenience store?

You are a depressed adolescent who sweats through her clothing and says terrible things to everyone, especially the people she loves.

You begin to lie. You have the urge to shoplift, and if you drive an automobile you have the urge to ram your car into the car in front of you.

Nothing can prepare you for this.

The one thing no one will tell you is that these feelings and this behavior will last ten years. That is, a decade of your life. Ask your doctor if this is true and she will deny it.

Then comes a day when you see a "woman" who is buying tampons and you think of her as a *girl*. And she is; anyone who has periods is a girl. You know this is true and it is very funny to you.

You are a woman, the ten years have passed, you love your children, you love your lover, but there are no longer any persons on earth who can stop you from being yourself— you have put your parents in the earth, you have buried the past. Of course in the meantime you have destroyed your life and it has to be completely remade and there is a great deal of grief and regret and nostalgia and all of that, but even so you are free, free to sit on the bank and throw stones and feel thankful for the few years or one or two decades left to you in which you can be yourself, even if a great many other women ended their lives, even if the reason they ended their lives is reported as having been for reasons having nothing to do with menopause, which is thankfully behind you as you would never want to be a girl again for any reason at all, you have discovered that being *invisible* is the biggest secret on earth, the most wondrous gift anyone could ever have given you.

If you are young and you are reading this, perhaps you will understand the gleam in the eye of any woman who is sixty, seventy, eighty, or ninety: she cannot take you seriously (sorry) for you are but a girl to her, despite your babies and shoes and lovemaking and all of that. You are just a girl playing at life.

You are just a girl on the edge of a great forest. You should be frightened but instead you are eating a lovely meal, or you are cooking one, or you are running to the florist or you are opening a box of flowers that has just arrived at your door—and none of these things is done in the great spirit that they will later be done in.

You haven't even begun. You must pause first, the way one must always pause before a great spirit, if only to take a good breath.

Happy old age is coming on bare feet, bringing with it grace and gentle words, and ways that grim youth has never known.

LULLABY

I did not attend my first concert of classical music until I was eighteen. The concert was in a small chapel high in the Swiss Alps, and there were so many people packed in under that roof it felt claustrophobic, but at least I had a bench to sit on—I suppose you'd call it a pew. After about fifteen minutes of listening to the music I fell asleep. I wasn't bored, I was relaxed, and, I suppose, happy (I've never been able to figure out how happiness feels). When the concert was over I woke up and was embarrassed to have been sleeping. The audience was on its way out. Have you ever noticed how after a performance the floor is littered with programs? An hour before, when the concert began, everyone wanted their program, everyone held their program with both hands and would not dream of letting it go, but afterwards people leave them on the empty seats, where they slip quietly to the floor. That has always made me sad. And so on my way out I picked up one of the abandoned programs from the floor. *Brahms's Lullabies*—that was the whole concert! Suddenly I felt that perhaps by falling asleep I was the only one who had truly *heard* the music! Of course I felt this to make myself feel better—feelings are strange that way. Brahms's lullabies. I slipped the program into my bag, as a memento of a lovely nap, and left the chapel. Outside it was cold and so starry that I stood there for a while looking up. Of that night, I remember the stars more than the music, but I remember that while looking up at the stars I was thinking of the programs scattered on the floor. I can't say that Brahms is one of my favorite composers, but one artist I have always loved is Giacometti, the Swiss sculptor and painter; when I look at his work I can see the tension everyone talks about, yet his work has always made me extraordinarily calm, as Brahms did that evening: as if everything, stretched out in infinite silence and space, were part of this big drawing, and his drawings were part of this big drawing, which was so big that to see the whole thing would put anyone to sleep—I mean you would lose consciousness. Giacometti, my lullaby. Henry Miller is another artist who can put you to sleep. I often fall asleep while reading him. When he uses that hard word *cunt* again and again, it finally becomes something soft, so very soft, which is startling because a cunt really *is* soft, it's a warm, soft, wet-while-young place, a *spot* really, given the size of the universe, the way a star is a spot, but there are so many of them—I mean cunts—who can keep track? Henry Miller himself has pointed this out, and so Henry Miller becomes bored and disenchanted and excited at the same time, and that is an interesting thing; if you want to go to sleep but the lullaby *excites* you, what can you do, I mean really, what can you do? You can listen to Brahms, you can look at Giacometti, you can read Henry Miller, but each will tell you in his own way that there is nothing, absolutely nothing, but the stars looking down on you, even when you think you are looking up. How heavy-handed I feel just writing this, how heavy my hand feels, how heavy my eyes, my very hair is dragging me down, but it is a truth and if you sleep through a truth you will but wake at the bitter end.

TAKE FRANK

Take Frank. Frank is a bright boy, yet a lazy and stubborn high school student, one who holds in disdain all of his teachers, especially the dedicated, passionate ones. All of his English teachers, since at least the seventh grade, have been passionate. They have all told Frank that if he would only read this or that book he would fall in love with it, he would find himself hidden between its pages, he would have his "mind blown away." Frank does not like the idea of having his mind blown away, he finds it suicidal; Frank likes his mind the way it is and he intends to keep it. Frank does not want to fall in love, nor to see himself or find himself, he sees himself every day and he finds himself fine, he is exactly who he is and wants to be. He does not understand what all the fuss is about. So when Mr. Pacquette, his English teacher, approached Frank and offered a way for Frank to make up his missing credit, Frank was not even vaguely interested. In Frank's view, things existed or did not exist, and things that did not exist could not be said to be missing; he lacked a certain amount of credit, that was a fact, but the credit had not gone missing, it simply did not exist. Why go looking for something that did not exist? His nonexistent credit was not a teenager who had been abducted, or was lost in the woods, there was no picture of it that could be nailed near the bus stop, it was not a cat, he did not care or have feelings for this thing that was, supposedly, missing. He, himself, had no sense of loss, it was Mr. Pacquette who had a sense of loss; passionate people, Frank had observed, had above all else a sense of loss. He knew this was somehow connected to their enthusiasm, their hysterical insistence, their waving about of their arms. Mr. Pacquette did in fact wave his arms about when he told Frank that he had found "the perfect assignment," that all Frank had to do was read Herman Melville's short story "Bartleby, the Scrivener" and write a short paper on it, and all the missing credit would be restored, while at the same time Frank's mind would be blown away—apparently this was a bonus. Frank was not interested and said so, he said "I would prefer not to," which Mr. Pacquette recognized instantly as the famous, and only, words of Bartleby the scrivener, though Frank did not recognize them as belonging to anyone other than himself, they were his own words, they had just left his mouth hadn't they? Yet

Frank's words only caused Mr. Pacquette to wave his arms more wildly, and Frank could see his teacher was on the verge of having a *point*, another thing Frank couldn't care less about and did not want to be privy to. So when Mr. Pacquette began to get even more excited, when he opened his mouth more widely than was humanly necessary and said "That's just the *point!*" Frank said "I'd prefer not to" and left the room. Which left the passionate English teacher alone in sad thought, thinking of all the missed connections and opportunities in life, of all the failures. He felt sorry for Frank, and for Herman Melville, and for Bartleby, and for himself; he felt sorry for the sad fate of literature, which should be able to save the world but can't, through no fault of its own. Meanwhile Frank was walking home along the railroad tracks, the sun shone down on him, his mind was intact, he was doing exactly what he wanted to be doing, he was in his own world, free, not trapped between the pages of a book, and if he saw an insect he could squash it under his foot, or he could save it in a matchbox he carried in his pocket for that purpose.

RECOLLECTIONS OF MY CHRISTMAS TREE

I have always been vulnerable when confronted with Christmas decorations, and I am sitting in my living room staring at them. The lights on the tree are blinking on and off and I'm mesmerized. I have never been to a hypnotist but maybe mesmerization is the last state you enter before going over the edge into hypnosis. Maybe being mesmerized is the last thing you remember. It does seem to be a state all its own. When I was a child I did the same thing—watched the lights blink on and off, alone in the living room at night. The only difference is I know a lot more about Christmas now than I did then. I knew practically nothing then. My mother put an electric candle in each window, they were ivory-colored plastic, and at the end of each taper, near the bulb, fake drips of wax were molded; I loved the drips the most, it meant that the candles looked real to people inside the house, not just to people looking at them from the outside. What I didn't know then was that these decorations evolved from the Jewish menorah, the Hebrew festival of lights. I don't think my mother knew that either, but if she did she never mentioned it. And I certainly never contemplated the resemblance of a sleigh to a cradle. A sleigh is basically a very large cradle. The runners of the sleigh are what makes the cradle rock. Once there was a very eccentric man, in the nineteenth century in upstate New York, and when he was in his fifties he had a carpenter build him a cradle. I saw it in a museum, the biggest cradle ever made, and every night he slept in it, and when he entered his last illness he stayed in the cradle day and night, feeling the sensual throes of the cradle while somebody nursed and rocked him. I mean in the sense of caring for him. He died in his cradle, and the card on the wall of the museum said he was happy at the end. When I was a child one of my ornaments was a little red velveteen sleigh. I used to put a tiny doll in it, but now it is empty. I don't even like it anymore and when I was decorating the tree I thought about throwing it away but then I remembered the man in the cradle and decided to keep it. My mother and father also decorated the outside of our house with lights. We lived in a different house every year, so it wasn't easy — the length of the light strings kept changing. People who live in the same house every year don't think about things like that, their dimensions stay the same, there's no need to adjust anything, ever. After the lights were up on the outside of the house, my father would put us in the car and drive around the neighborhood, looking at the lights on the other houses. Sometimes he made disparaging remarks and sometimes in silence admired them. When he admired them he would make changes in his own lights the following year, but as we were by then in a new house none of the neighbors knew we were copycats. The most beautiful yard we ever saw had a snow scene with a frozen pond in the middle and life-sized figure skaters who floated across the pond wearing muffs. This was in Southern California, so everything was fake—the snow, the frozen pond, even the skaters were fake, and when they moved you could hear a slight whir under the ice—I guess it came from a motor. My father couldn't copy that—I could tell from his face that he was defeated. In those days everyone had lights. Not a single house was without them. That's one thing that has certainly changed. Today, only poor people have lights, and the poorest people of all have the most of them. At least this is true of the town I live in. There is one street that has the poorest people of all and at Christmas it is ablaze with lights, there are electric deer on the lawns and huge inflatable Santas, the roofs have more Santas descending in sleighs with reindeer, that kind of thing. The rich people think it is ugly, they don't bother anymore and they worry about the electric bill. They try to live calm, natural lives. They bake all their own bread, they make cookies and cakes and pies from scratch, they make their own beer and their own wine and liquors and they grow their own food in the summer—and come winter, when they want a Christmas tree or some holly, they just walk out on their land and cut it. Poor people have to use money, they have to go to the store and buy food, especially the kind that is already made. It didn't used to be that way. When I was a kid, it was understood that poor people had to make everything themselves while rich people got to buy things. My mother bought whole cakes at the grocery store and said we were lucky, not to have to make them ourselves. Now everything is reversed. If my mother and father were still alive they would be very confused. I think we would all become confused, eventually, if we didn't die. Maybe death prevents a major confusion that would, if it were allowed to go on, eventually kill us all. When I was little, one Christmas ritual majorly confused me. My mother had a little ceramic sleigh that sat on the table. It was driven by a ceramic Santa and pulled by ceramic reindeer. Every year I had to wrap empty matchboxes so they looked like tiny presents. Then we piled them in the sleigh; they were the presents Santa was hauling. But they were empty, and it made me sad. My mother would sit at the table smoking, watching me wrap the matchboxes. Can't we put anything in them? I asked. No, she said, they're fake. Couldn't we pretend? I said. That's what we're doing, she said. I mean *real pretend*, I said, but she just stared off into space and I knew the conversation had ended. One thing is for certain—I wouldn't want to be a Christmas tree. It would be nice to be the center of attention, to be so decorated and lit that people stared at you in wonder, and made a fuss over you, and were mesmerized. That would be nice. But then you'd start dropping your needles and people would become bored with you and say you weren't looking so good, and then they'd take off all your jewelry, and haul you off to the curb where you would be picked up and crushed and eventually burned. That's the terrible part. Maybe that's why so many people today have fake trees. They are quite popular. Their limbs come apart and you can put them in boxes and store them. You can have one of these trees until you die and you can pass it on to your children. They may not be real but when you look at them you can't tell the difference. That always makes people happy—not being able to tell the difference. And happiness, to want to be happy, is the most natural thing of all. That man in his big cradle was happy, though I never understood why, when he died, they didn't just saw the runners off and use it as his coffin. I don't think anyone would have noticed; in the end, the difference between a cradle and a coffin is hardly worth mentioning, though then again I wouldn't have seen the cradle later, in the museum, and if that hadn't happened I wouldn't have kept my red velveteen sleigh, I would have just thrown it away. No, never! When it comes to Christmas, when Christmas comes, I sit firmly on the lap of Charles Dickens, and repeat after him: Welcome, Everything! At this well-remembered time, when Everything is capable, with the greatest of ease, of being changed into Anything. On this day we shut out Nothing!

Purple sadness is the sadness of classical music and egg-plant, the stroke of midnight, human organs, ports cut off for part of every year, words with too many meanings, incense, insomnia, and the crescent moon. It is the sadness of play money, and icebergs seen from a canoe. It is possible to dance to purple sadness, though slowly, as slowly as it takes to dig a pit to hold a sleeping giant. Purple sadness is pervasive, and goes deeper into the interior than the world's greatest nickel deposits, or any other sadness on earth. It is the sadness of depositories, and heels echoing down a long corridor, it is the sound of your mother closing the door at night, leaving you alone.

Black sadness is the ashling, its remains are scattered over several provinces, it is the sadness of rakes and hyphenated names, of clouds who think they are grapes, it is the sadness of brooches, which may be worn on the breast or at the neck but how sad none see the sadness of detail there, the woman playing a guitar without strings, the hare leaping from the fox in vain, it is sadness torn and sadness rent, it is the hole in sadness from which no words escape and no soul can spring, it is the calorific sadness of bombs. Many of us used to own a black velvet skirt. It is little Angie Moss on her way to the fair, it is there she will have her first adventure.

ONE GIRL'S THEORY

Mr. Timothy Wells was killed in an instant by fallen timber at the raising of a large barn, 18th October, a clear day, no tuft in our sky. For Thy information he was 28 years of age and after the accident his eyes remained open. After reading that, I had to leave the graveyard. How you bait your hooks is immoral. I didn't want to think about it so I stopped for lunch in a joint off the lake and was seated in a booth next to the window. The window had lace curtains, the curtains had acorns and oak leaves woven into them. I was served a glass of water, one bowl of pea soup, and a pair of saltines packaged together. Two people in the next booth were talking. Billions and billions of years in the future, said one. Billions and billions of years ago, said the other. It made me sad so I left, leaving the saltine packaging next to a nifty tip. What were those people talking about? Once I imagined a baby born with eight or nine hearts on a planet with as many moons, but that wasn't nearly enough. Fishing boats bobbed along the edges of the lake. There didn't seem to be anyone listening to them. Once in Thy wisdom (a long time ago, in

England) you caused a baby to be born without a brain. It lived a few days then the doctors lit into it, that's when they found the empty space in its skull. None believe this true story, their brains won't let them. But I think this babe was your love child, and everyone who reads about him, you kill.

TO A MAGAZINE

I am rejecting your request for a letter of rejection. One must reject everything in order to live. That may be true, but the rejected know another knowledge—that if they were not rejected, heaven would descend upon the earth in earthly dreams and an infinite flowering of all living forms would form a silveresque film over our sordid history, which has adventitiously progressed through violent upheavals in reaction to rejection; without rejection there would be no as-we-know-it Earth. What is our ball but a rejected stone flung from the mother lode? The rejected know that if they were nonrejected a clear cerulean blue would be the result, an endless love ever dissolving in more endless love. This is their secret, and none share it save them. They remain, therefore, the unbelieved, they remain the embodiment of heaven herself. Let others perpetuate life as we know it—that admixture, that amalgam, the happy, the sad, the profusion of all things under the sunny moon existing in a delicate balance, such as it is. Alone, the rejected walk a straight path, they enter a straight gate, they see in their dreams what no one else can see—an end to all confusion, an end to all suffering, an elysian mist of eternally good vapor. Forgive me if I have put your thoughts into words. It was the least I could do for such a comrade, whose orphaned sighs reach me in my squat hut.

MILKSHAKE

I am never lonely, and never bored. Except when I bore myself, which is my definition of loneliness—to bore oneself. It makes a body lonesome, that. Today I am very bored, and very lonely. I can think of nothing better to do than grind salt and pepper into my milkshake, which I have been doing since I was thirteen, which was so long ago the very word *thirteen* has an old-fashioned ring to it, one might as well say "Ottoman Empire." Traditionally, thirteen is an unlucky number. Little did I know at thirteen that I was on the road, by a single action, to loneliness and boredom. My friend Vicki and I were sitting at the lunch counter in Woolworth's, waiting for the milkshakes we had ordered—hers chocolate, mine vanilla—when she got up to go to the ladies' room. The chocolate shake came while she was gone and as a joke I sprinkled salt and pepper on it, because I was, though I didn't know it, young and callous and cruel. Vicki came back, she took the paper off her straw, she stuck her straw in her milkshake, she sucked through the straw for what seemed an eternity, and then she swallowed, which seemed like forever. *This is the best milkshake I have ever had.* That's what she said, though she didn't say it as much as she sighed it. *The best shake I've ever had.* In such sudden and unexpected ways does boredom begin. I tried her milkshake, I told her what I had done, the vanilla shake came and we salt-and-peppered that one, too, and afterwards we were bored, so we went shopping — we were in Woolworth's after all — though by shopping we meant shoplifting, as any lonely bored thirteen-year-old knows. Vicki stole a little tub of the latest invention, lip gloss, which was petroleum jelly dyed pink, and I stole a yellow lace mantilla to wear to Mass on Easter Sunday, though I never wore it to Mass: I wore it to confession the Saturday before, confessing to the priest that I had stolen the very thing I was wearing on my head. Why not? I had nothing else to confess. Playing a mean trick on my best friend, even one that turned out all right, didn't seem worth the bother. What bothered me was that the priest seemed bored by my confession; I had thought to shock him, but it was he who shocked me, as I had so little experience of adult boredom. He gave me three Hail Marys and closed the screen. What was happening? I had shocked myself by stealing the mantilla and then confessing it, but bored the priest, whose boredom now shocked me, though it would bore me later, years later, when lip gloss was as common as clover, when the idea of Catholic women covering their heads was antiquated, when priests were suspected of being callous and cruel, and the combination of salt and sugar was a raging trend, served in all the swank joints and upscale places. But, as I said, I am never lonely and never bored, and if today is an exception, it is the age-old exception of every day, for every day turns into tomorrow, and tomorrow turns into today, and today into yesterday, and I confess there is very little any of us can do to change it.

Gray sadness is the sadness of paper clips and rubber bands, of rain and squirrels and chewing gum, ointments and unguents and movie theaters. Gray sadness is the most common of all sadnesses, it is the sadness of sand in the desert and sand on the beach, the sadness of keys in a pocket, cans on a shelf, hair in a comb, dry-cleaning, and raisins. Gray sadness is beautiful, but not to be confused with the beauty of blue sadness, which is irreplaceable. Sad to say, gray sadness is replaceable, it can be replaced daily, it is the sadness of a melting snowman in a snowstorm.

Red sadness is the secret one. Red sadness never appears sad, it appears as Nijinsky bolting across the stage in mid-air, it appears in flashes of passion, anger, fear, inspiration, and courage, in dark unsellable visions; it is an upside-down penny concealed beneath a tea cozy, the even-tempered and steady-minded are not exempt from it, and a curator once attached this tag to it: *Because of the fragile nature of the pouch no attempt has been made to extract the note.*

AMONG THE CLOUDS

That was the summer there were so many clouds we didn't know what to do with them. They overflowed the sky — they were on our streets, in our homes, in our drawers, and in our cabinets. They were in our cars and on our buses, I even saw them in taxis. No one had ever seen so many clouds, to the extent that, as often happens with a glut, no one could remember a time without them. Our legislators tried to ship them to another country, but the question came back — what would one do with so many clouds? There was no wind, no rain, nothing to break them up or break off the endless building up of them. Ship them to Mars, someone said; but Mars could not sustain them. You needed an atmosphere for that, and how odd was that, since so many clouds clouded our atmosphere and every citizen felt they were in a play, at the theater, overcome by another's mood, at the mercy of the infinite nostalgia of subconscious dictates. I was not the first to be surprised and often terrified by their images. They cast long shadows in an unearthly light. Some were blue, some were gray, some black, some white, some were pink, some were lavender, some orange, some a ghastly purple. All cast a trance and a silence upon us. I registered without choice the complaints of a multitude. Our dreams of a solution, even the most obscure, dissolved in the profound and vital roots of an intractable reality. The picture of a limp cloud watching us was undeniable. They were irrational, impossible, baffling and alarming, solitary, in strata, stippled as a fish's back, fantastically shaped, and plain as the day is long. They hypnotized us and paralyzed us. Yet they remained, in the highest and lowest places, and the meticulous exact realism of them convinced us to capture them, and zoo them, and feed them, to the extent others, far into the researchable future, would be able to see what was the temporary but encroaching weight of their total reality, and perhaps understand our hopelessness of ever understanding them, why they were so crowded among us, given we were crowned with brains to override them, which proved impossible, though there are so few left who remember. Even now, so many years later, when strolling idly, say on a Sunday, under a spotless sky, when I meet a child carrying in her right hand, like a torch, a tuft of spun sugar on a stick, the familiar cry of that summer comes back to me, the one that floated out of the mouths of so many children: *O Mother, O Father, wherefore art thou? I cannot see to find thee among so many clouds.*

MY PRIVATE PROPERTY

It is sad, is it not, that no one today displays any interest in the art of shrunken heads. Men, women, and children walk on streets, they cross fields and enter forests, they run along the edges of oceans, but none of them, to the best of my knowledge, are thinking about shrunken heads. I am thinking about shrunken heads, but keep the thought to myself, that is, inside my head, for if the subject is raised at all, it is met with horror, on account of the violence involved in the necessary removal of the head before you can shrink it. But as an art and a conception, the tribes of the Amazon displayed a genius that deserves our awe; miniaturizing and preserving a human head is a glory and wonder on the scale of the Great Pyramids. I recently encountered a passage on shrunken heads in *Kon-Tiki*, the best-selling account by Thor Heyerdahl of his journey, with five companions, on a simple wooden raft that set sail from the coast of Peru in 1947 and landed on an uninhabited South Sea island 101 days later. The journey, which even professional mariners thought would end in disaster, was undertaken to prove Heyerdahl's theory that Polyne-

sia was settled by peoples of the South American conti-
nent. It is not a book that is much read today, but the copy
I found at the Goodwill was in its 21st printing in 1962,
so it is fair to think that for many years people did think
about shrunken heads, which are mentioned in passing
on page 62. By 1947, when Heyerdahl and his men were
building their raft in a naval yard in Lima, the market for
shrunken heads was strictly an illegal one, but there were
still people who made their living selling the desiccated
top portion of the human body. The Amazonian jungle
is very dense and such a thing is hard to control. Heyer-
dahl's account is brief and sketchy but one learns that it
is done like this: after the requisite decapitation, the skull
is smashed and removed through the neck, leaving the
skin of the head intact, like a sack of flesh, which is then
filled with hot sand, which causes the sack to shrink with-
out losing its shape or any of its features. The shrunken
head is about the size of an orange. One of Thor's men,
who had lived in the jungle a long time, had a friend who
was murdered and whose head was shrunk; a promise was
made to spare the murderers in exchange for the head,
and so the little head was eventually handed to its widow,
who fainted. Thereafter it was kept in a trunk where it

mildewed and from time to time had to be hung by its hair on a clothesline and left in the air to dry. Every time its widow saw it, she fainted. One day a mouse got into the trunk and that was the end of the head. To be eaten by a mouse! To be eaten by worms is charmless and inevitable. But for your head to be nibbled at by a mouse, for your head to become a bit of moldy cheese on a plate — that was something that spoke volumes about reversals of power, about foolishness and vanity. It reminded me of a nineteenth-century Japanese drawing I had once seen — *Mice transcribing a book,* by Kawanabe Kyosai — in which red-eyed white mice wearing kimonos are kneeling at a low desk transcribing a book, while off in the corner naked black mice are devouring the pages of a previously transcribed book. Am I vain to think of my head as a book? Am I not transcribing the book of my head as I write? To be eaten by a mouse! I had to learn more, so I did some research and found a more detailed account of how it is done, a method used by the Jivaro Indians of the Ecuadoran and Peruvian Amazon, who, as far as I can tell, are known today as the Shuar; these ethnocentricities become amazingly complicated. The Jivaro, or Shuar, slit the head-flesh up the back to remove the skull, throwing the skull in the river to appease the river gods. The eyes and the mouth are sewn shut, to paralyze the spirit, which, having died violently, would be bent on revenge. The flesh-head is boiled for two hours until the skin is dark and rubbery and one-third its original size. The skin is then turned inside out and any flesh still sticking to the inside is scraped off, then the head is inverted back and by this time resembles an empty rubber glove. The final shrinking is done with sand, and hot stones dropped one at a time through the neck opening, constantly rotated inside to prevent scorching. The sand enters the places the stones cannot, the crevices of the nose and ears, and hot stones are applied to the exterior, too, to seal and shape the features. Surplus hair is singed off and the finished product hung over a fire to harden and blacken. A heated machete is applied to the lips to dry them, and then they are lashed together with native fiber. The word for shrunken heads is *tsantsa* (pronounced *san-sah*), and the process has been in existence for as long as anyone can remember, an art so old it has no known origin. It takes about a week to shrink a head, the artist working daily. A ceremony follows where a string is inserted in the head so it can be worn around the neck, for the head of the enemy is a trophy, a living trophy of sorts, for it contains the spirit of the vanquished. Some tribes, though, didn't keep the heads after the ceremony but fed them to animals or gave them to children as a plaything to be lost. In this instance, they are dolls, but with a difference — they are *real* dolls, every girl's dream. It is hard to fake a shrunken head, but once they became a commodity — enter the white man — many tried. Some clever folk used other animals altogether, such as the heads of monkeys and goats. Where there is value, there will be experts, and experts say that nose hair and ears are especially hard to fake. An expert examining a shrunken head to determine whether or not it is *real* is not unlike an art expert examining a supposed Rembrandt to determine whether or not it is *real*: magnifying glasses are used. But I keep thinking about the mouse, who didn't care or know whether the head was anything other than a real meal. We eat jerky don't we? Most of all, I like the idea that a head can continue to have a fate after it's dead. And the story of the widow who fainted every time she saw her husband's head on the clothesline took me back to my own first encounter with a shrunken head. When I was sixteen years old and in school in Brussels I would very often play hooky, skipping school it is also called, and always when I did I did the same thing, I took a tram to the outskirts of the city and wandered through that marble mausoleum commonly called the Congo Museum. I may not have been a writer at sixteen, but I was most emphatically a daydreamer, and felt deliriously happy to be free, wandering under the hanging canoes, staring at the stuffed elephants and peering into the eyeholes of masks, with which I felt a special relationship. Of course I am filled with retrospective shame, but not for my feeling of freedom, freedom is something one should never feel ashamed of, but for my sheer and utter ignorance; I can now say that my ignorance was not in any way caused by my absence from the classroom, I can assure you my school did not teach what I now know to be true—that the museum I wandered in was built on rape and plunder and pillage and oppression and murder, that everything in it was stolen, that the very wealth necessary for such acquisition was stolen, wealth acquired by force of so filthy and unspeakable an evil our heads cannot fathom it and have no single word for it, but must resort to endless corridors of words, each corridor turning into another corridor a thousand miles longer than the last in our hopeless search for some inner chamber of understanding that does not exist. Among these millions of words time passes, and in time slavery passes, if only on paper, a page shuffled among thousands of pages, and then there are two words, *rubber* and *ivory*, that break off from the others and river around the world in the forms of automobile tires and piano keys. But commerce and culture quickly take us down a corridor leading to more automobile tires and more piano keys, and their equivalent—money—and I want to go the way of shrunken heads, and dolls, soft rubbery flesh and ivory-like porcelain, skin and bones, faces and masks. At sixteen, I was not much the other side of dolldom, so it is little wonder that there in the Congo Museum I fell in love with a shrunken head. Of course, the head was not Amazonian but African. I don't know how the art evolved on that continent, but genius flourishes everywhere, it has always been so and will always be so, and there will always be people who believe otherwise. As I said, a shrunken head is as close to a *real* doll as one could ever come, and in this sense it is both a child's toy and an adult toy— it's another person after all—and I was not then, nor am I now, immune to the charms of having someone else to play with. He was dangling from an invisible thread, much as a spider does, from the top of a glass case taller than I was. He *was* the size of an orange. He was particular and unique and human and utterly real, a man with eyes and eyelashes and hair (apparently the Africans do not close the eyes of their dolls). It was only later that I learned that the hair and eyelashes do not shrink with the flesh of the face, and so the shrunken often have the luxurious eyelashes of a child, and the hair is much longer than the face, though often cut, so great is the human impulse toward proportion. But my man had long, uncut hair, and as it was 1969 I didn't think anything of it; all the men I liked had long, uncut hair. His skin had the sheen of an eggplant—it must have been oiled—and all the purples of that fruit were in it; his nose was broad and flat, his eyes deeply set, unnaturally so, and beautifully shining, but so many years have passed I cannot be sure of what was there and what was not, though I returned to look at him countless times; he was, after a while, what I came to look at, and at some point I began to commune with him. Yes, I gave life to an inanimate object, but can a human head ever really be said to be an inanimate object? He was not a skull, he was not decomposing, he was not mangled in any way. He had been, and *was*, a person. I don't remember what it was we communed about, but he possessed me as I possessed him, and to possess the head of a beloved, no less than the head of an enemy, is the greatest sickness on earth. I could enter the museum blindfolded and turn exactly the right corners, one after another, to find myself standing before him at eye-level. I shall never forget his expression: he looked *startled*. No other words come to mind. And though I could not see myself, I must have looked startled, too. We stood facing each other the way, when you come upon a deer unexpectedly, you both freeze for a moment, mutually startled, and in that exchange there seems to be but one glance, as if you and the other are sharing the same pair of eyes. The years passed. I left the city, I never returned, the signage in the museum changed, of that I am sure, but the impression left upon me by the shrunken head has never changed, so that I now wonder why human beings do not incorporate the art of shrinking heads into their burial rites. I am serious. What prevents us from saving the heads of the dead we bury, since we can make them the size of oranges (or apples), and keeping them, out of the deepest love and respect, for our descendants, for whom the heads will become ancestors, for what are ancestors but *the loved ones of our loved ones,* since a single act of love, down through the ages, has procured what we call the future? I am presuming, of course, that procreation involves love, which it very often does not, and so I hesitate to say love is the greatest traveler, I could just as easily say sex; perhaps love is but symbolic behavior toward sex—it is certainly symbolic behavior toward the living and the dead. I am most interested in shrunken heads as symbolic behavior toward the dead. Marks of being a human involve symbolic behavior toward the dead; no other animal does it to the extent humans do. Don't we carry photographs of the heads of those we love who have died? Don't we frame their heads and keep them on the mantel as reminders of all that is precious and binds us to this life? And before there were photographs, that rage of the well-to-do, that sign of commerce and culture, there were hand-painted miniatures (if you could afford them), exquisitely detailed renditions of the head, kept in a protective locket or box that could be carried inside a jacket or coat. Someone leaving on a long journey would carry such a head. A Belgian officer or intrepid explorer would carry such a head into the African jungle. Surely Commandant Dhanis (afterwards Baron), making his way toward Katanga, carried such a head, and surely from time to time he took it out of his coat or jacket and looked at it. And his heart was filled with love, even if that love did not extend to the foliage around him, nor to the people whose habitat it was, several of whom were artists in shrinking heads, no less than the miniaturist. The human heart is hard to fathom, no less than the human head. They both contribute to human behavior, the hardest of all to fathom. I don't know when psychiatrists and psychologists were first called *shrinks*, but the term has stuck. I confess I don't understand it myself, for my personal experience with psychotherapy is that it expands the head in wondrous ways, it educates the mind to view itself, and others, from new perspectives amounting to vistas. There is nothing small about it. I first began seeing a shrink after the death of my mother. I was then in my midforties and considered myself highly intelligent. A large part of my intelligence depended on my total ignorance of how ignorant I really was. I was not unlike Commandant Dhanis, the Belgian aristocrat who carried a miniature head into the jungle without realizing the Congolese were far superior in that art. Even today, when I muse about preserving the heads of loved ones by postmortem shrinkage, I am ignorant; I seldom stop to consider the obstacles and absurdities of my plan. My mother's head, for example, could not have been shrunk by any means, as she died from injuries sustained in a gruesome accident, which resulted in her head, during the few remaining weeks of her life, swelling to inhuman proportions. My mother's head went, rather quickly, from the size of a head to the size of a watermelon to the size of a prizewinning pumpkin. It was impossible to look at it (her) unless you pretended you were watching a horror film and that it wasn't real, but was a giant grotesque doll created by special effects. At least that is how I remember enduring one such viewing. Unlike a shrunken head, when a human head is enlarged it cannot sustain its features, the eyes and the nose and the mouth all disappear in one gigantic gelatinous mass; such a head does not remotely resemble the person it belongs to. So much so, I pinned a photograph of my mother over her hospital bed so that the doctors and nurses might know what their patient looked like. It seems strange to me now, the gesture of that photograph, as none of the medical staff knew her before her accident, and there was no hope at any time that her head would deflate to recognizable proportions. I think I pinned that photograph up for myself, so I could remember her as I knew her. No, my mother's head, sadly, could not have been shrunk, by even the greatest artist, and yet her head has always figured into my daydream of having twelve shrunken heads, each one belonging to someone who has passed through my life, touching me in deep and unforgettable ways, and I would keep my dozen heads in an egg carton made especially for them, twelve beloved heads kept safe and together. I would never let them mold or rot, I would not let the mice near them, their fate would be to remain exactly as they were in life, exactly as they *are*, albeit orange-sized and portable, and from time to time I would take them out and look at them and be startled, and I think of the widow who fainted at the sight of her husband's head, and I think if I could hold the head of a single beloved in my hand I would indeed feel faint, but I think also I would get used to it, I would grow calm and be moved in the tenderest of ways, just the sight of them there in my hand, resting gently and safely (a shrunken head cannot be broken) with such tiny and shining eyes, why, resting gently and safely with such tiny and shining eyes it would be as if they were but babies, returning to live again, and I could touch their faces. I am ashamed to think of the baby heads as my private property, but I do. It has been said that inside the human head is to be found the only freedom that exists for all, but very often that freedom grows lonely and bored and frightened and yearns to join another head, very often owning one head is not enough, owning your own head gives rise to the desire for the head of another, out of the perfectly natural desire for love and communion. But out of greed, out of the desire for control and power, grows a monster, the desire to own as many heads as possible. None of us are immune—who doesn't want more clients, patients, customers, readers—but desire can swell to inhuman proportions. Thus the King of Belgium declared a vast territory as his private property, and all heads within it, including (unbeknownst to him) all the shrunken heads, heads shrunk after a week's worth of artful work. I don't really know anything about heads, though I spend a disproportionate amount of my time thinking about them, and more time than ever since seeing a shrink. I am not even sure I own my own head, but my innermost fantasy is to own twelve beloved heads nestled in an egg carton, to comfort me in moments of dearth in exchange for my infinite love. How can I call myself benevolent? I want, as my personal private property, twelve human heads. I have often thought god needs prayers to remind himself he is important, and still matters. Without our interceding glances, what would he be but a shrunken head on the end of a thread in a museum of ideas? Sometimes I think there is no place left for me to go but back to the Congo Museum, that horrific monument of smashed lies and beautiful things, and stand face-to-face before a face I can barely remember but do, and pray to that shriveled thing that when I die, as I must, let someone preserve me as I was then, that first day, ignorant, innocent, at my most beautiful, and overcome by another. It occurs to me I wanted to die that day. Why else would I have skipped school and wandered off alone and found a friend among the dead? One who thrilled me to life? O my pantheon of shrunken heads, struck like new-laid eggs in a carton, comfort me when my rivers are high, comfort me when my waters are gone, for I can almost hear you breathing.

OLD IMMORTALITY

The Earl of Staffordshire was the least eccentric of his ancestral line; one of his forebears had died after eating horse manure in the belief it would cure him of jealousy, a belief we cannot deny proved true in the end. The present Earl had no intention of dying, he sought in its place the immortality of art, specifically that of the writer, specifically that of his rival, Sir Walter Scott, whose Waverly novels were being read by everyone in the shire who could read. Their anonymity had long been dispelled, the year was 1815, and the Earl of Staffordshire, of whom we speak, set out to write a sequel to his favorite, *Old Mortality*, and gave his book the title *Old Immortality* without having yet written a single word. But write he did, by day and by night, behind heavy curtains, by the light of six tapers, and with a curious nib at the end of his quill, a gold nib specially made from his wife's golden wedding ring, she having died in childbirth along with his heir some thirty years previous. The Earl found he could not quite sustain the life of a novelist and the novel ended after only eighty pages, and of the tale we shall only say that its greatest merit was how profoundly it illustrated the old adage *It is a long lane that has no turning.* The Earl was nonetheless satisfied he had by his own hand acquired immortality, or if he had his doubts, they were as heavily curtained as his chambers. We would not be writing his story, even as simply and briefly as we mean to state it, if in fact he had not attained what he sought, though not quite in the manner of his original vision. Our Earl could have paid any price in England to ensure his book saw print, but hit upon a plan whose novelty became legend, giving *Old Immortality* its place in the cupboard of letters. He took the manuscript to the Staffordshire pottery, whose reputation, even at that time, was renowned among English potters, if not unsurpassed, and whose original wares reside today in museums the world over, and in the private collections of those individuals whose pressing passion is the historical significance of clay. The extra expense of securing the services of the pottery's master modeler, John Hackwood, was to our Earl equivalent to the effort of waving away a summer fly landed on the edge of his teacup. The plan was simple: one hundred four dining plates, bearing in sequence the text of his novel, including the title pages, author's preface, and an exquisite *finis* sheet embellished with garlands of eglantine, a last-minute inspiration designed to follow the page bearing the word *end*. Each plate was of bisque, a vitreous clay with a matte finish, and the color chosen was that of cream in the second hour of clotting. The plates were round, eleven inches in diameter with a slightly fluted edge but without a margin, in order to accommodate as many words as possible. On the underside was the mark of the pottery, the mark of the master modeler, John Hackwood, and a numeral designated to be both plate and page number. The text itself, modeled entirely by hand, in this case the hand of John Hackwood, was raised out of the bisque and given a jasper glaze, which in contrast to the bisque below provided easy readability. It is true the first sixty plates had to be destroyed, having been fired by an apprentice, but the Earl waved this expense off as if it were but the fly come back. *Old Immortality* took two days less than ten months to come to print, and the next step was for the Earl to present his book of plates to twenty-six esteemed guests invited to his table on the twenty-first of June 1816, for a seven-course banquet, the four central courses being reserved for the inaugural reading. The kitchen staff, in particular, spent the previous fortnight in rehearsal, for the guests were not to be simultaneously served, each guest being presented with food only after he had read his plate aloud to those assembled there for the occasion, and the food had to be kept hot behind the closed doors of the kitchen, and each footman, with perfect timing, fill each plate on the last breath of its recitation. Each guest needed to read four times, thus each guest needed to be presented with four different plates, set down at intervals as the evening, the meal, and the novel progressed. The Earl spared no expense, and provided his footmen with fresh gloves for each exchange of plates. It cannot be determined what was served that night, but we can imagine that after the soup bowls were cleared and the novel appeared, the quail came forth, the trout, the beef, the pastry filled with salmon, the Russian potatoes, the asparagus in aspic, all these and more perhaps, before the Earl held up his *finis* plate and the cheeses and pears and puddings were brought in. The wine flowed from start to finish, and if the chinatized literature did not go as smoothly, no one noticed, though it would perhaps be more accurate to record that no one spoke. What records we possess of the evening come down to us in the form of a review written by the Earl of

Staffordshire before retiring to his bed that very night, though in his vigor he neglected the viands and detailed only the glorious reception of his immortal work, as indicated by the twenty-six stunned and speechless faces; though he did note the Duchess of Langford wore an offensively large jewel, though this doubtless harked back to his unsuccessful courtship of her some thirty years previous. The Earl gave his novel banquet twelve times a year until his death, never inviting the same guest twice, ensuring himself the readership he had dared dream of. And what became of the book? What became of the plates, the beautiful plates gleaming under the candelabra on the long table, one hundred four served in succession, twelve to a side, one at the head and one at the foot, each plate a page, each page exemplifying further it is a long lane that has no turning? Alas, the beautiful plates were destroyed by the Earl's grandnephew, who, in 1870, under the influence of the Arts and Crafts movement, invited his friends to a banquet that rapidly became debauched, and sometime after midnight while our Earl slept in his grave in the family chapel less than a mile removed, the youthful crew, who fancied themselves visionaries, and under the influence of wine and chloral hydrate, broke the plates one by one, flinging them against the fireplace after a cursory reading, which eventually ceased as the breaking went on, which is when they began to recite from memory recently published verses of Dante Gabriel Rossetti, verses the poet had buried with his first wife and just this past October exhumed from her coffin, leaving the lady poemless in her doom. O cold, cruel shards of Immortality! Not a single one remains to be unearthed by the garden wall. Yet one complete plate remains extant, with a single hairline crack crossing its bisque skull, if we can so call a plate whereon a man's mind is mapped; it is the one bordered with tangled vines of eglantine, that wild rose of poetic repute, and as you have guessed, dear reader, it bears the word *finis*.

Green sadness is sadness dressed for graduation, it is the sadness of June, of shiny toasters as they come out of their boxes, the table laid before a party, the smell of new strawberries and dripping roasts about to be devoured; it is the sadness of the unperceived and therefore never felt and seldom expressed, except on occasion by polka dancers and little girls who, in imitation of their grandmothers, decide who shall have their bunny when they die. Green sadness weighs no more than an unused handkerchief, it is the funereal silence of bones beneath the green carpet of evenly cut grass upon which the bride and groom walk in joy.

Pink sadness is the sadness of white anchovies. It is the sadness of deprivation, of going without, of having to swallow when your throat is no bigger than an acupuncture pin; it's the sadness of mushrooms born with heads too big for their bodies, the sadness of having the soles come off your only pair of shoes, or your favorite pair, it makes no difference, pink sadness cannot be measured by a gameshow host, it is the sadness of shame when you have done nothing wrong, pink sadness is not your fault, and though even the littlest twinge may cause it, it is the vast bushy top on the family tree of sadness, whose faraway roots resemble a colossal squid with eyes the size of soccer balls.

IN THE FOREST

When I wander in the forest I am drawn towards language, I see meaning is quaintly hidden, shooting up in dark wet woods, by roots of trees, old walls, among dead leaves, strangely lonely, suggestive of some wild individuality, silently symbolical of old Vienna, but lacking in details. When I wander in the forest, I am afraid of getting lost, and I feel most strongly that something is waiting for me, under a fallen log, behind a tree, there in some high-up hole in the tree trunk, though I seldom look up, no, as I walk I look down, drawn to the root system as I stumble, and I don't think that it is Sanskrit waiting for me, not for a minute, I think *what time is it* and *shouldn't I be getting home*, one can't always be wandering in meaning, dark as it is it will be getting darker, though if it begins to snow I look up, I lose myself in the snow as it falls between branches and builds up also on every one, I lose myself just as my steps are beginning to leave tracks in the snow on the forest floor, and soon the fallen logs are covered with snow, and when my tracks are covered I am completely lost, the snow has muffled everything, and the silence frightens me as much as the forest ever did.

THE HOODED DREAM
OF DINING

Alice loved poetry. John loved poetry. Mary and Michael and Susan loved poetry. They went to a restaurant to sit together at a table and talk about the thing they loved. In walked David, who did not love poetry. He sat by himself at a small circular table, where he could hear other people talking but not what they were saying, and after he ordered he sat dreaming of mountaintops, of standing on a mountaintop looking down on the valley below, of watching a river snaking in the distance, of the wind in his hair. Still, being in a restaurant dreaming of mountaintops, he might as well have been fishing for pine needles. So David thought about his wife, who did not love poetry and did not love mountaintops, but loved red thread, which she collected for no reason and to no purpose. David thought of the time he stole a few strands from her desk and threw them in a stew he was making, to surprise her, but when he ladled the stew into her bowl and watched her eat it, it was apparent she didn't even notice. Still, a few hours later she seemed inexplicably happy, so he closed his eyes and thought of that.

LIKE A SCARF

For him, the affair was the flight of a weightless balloon borne by wind over a plaza. For her, the affair was the flight of a yellow silk scarf borne by the wind over the plaza, the rooftops of slanted tile, the highways, the beach, the rocky coastline and the inland forest; the scarf was thirty-three inches square with hand-rolled edges that had been rolled in Japan by the tiny fingers of Umi, a twenty-year-old worker in the silk district of Tomioka. Umi lived with her father, a widower, and after work in the factory returned home to care for him, preparing a meal of rice, eel, and radish, eating with him in silence, later burning incense in front of the household shrine, which contained a black-and-white photograph of her mother at the age of forty-two, a year before she died of cancer of the womb. Her last words had been spoken in a state of semiconsciousness, and it was unclear to whom they were addressed: *Let me.* The scarf whose edges Umi had rolled with her fingers was shipped to Milan to be sold in a department store, where it was bought by a man as a gift for his lover, who did not have the heart to tell him she never wore yellow (hadn't he noticed?) and the next day gave the scarf to her sister (who was delighted), telling her lover that the scarf had been blown off her head by a sudden gust of wind as she was crossing the plaza on her way to visit her sister, and though she was sorry to lose it, it had been the most beautiful sight (he should have been there), many heads tilted upwards to follow its path as it billowed across a cloudless lavender sky (he should have been there), it really was the most unexpected sight, one of the pedestrians even said out loud *Look, a balloon!* and later, at the dentist, the pedestrian described again that moment of grace, and the dentist listened very carefully as he injected Novocain into the man's gums, so carefully that later that evening he remembered to tell his wife about the flight of the balloon, which she instantly recognized because she had been there, she told her husband how she was crossing the plaza on her way to buy a pair of shoes when she saw it, a sight so beautiful she had wanted to take a video with her phone, but by the time she found her phone at the bottom of her bag the scarf was gone; still, the sight of the yellow silk scarf sailing over the plaza had so arrested her she no longer felt like buying shoes, and sat instead at a table at an outdoor café, order-

ing an aperitif of such a vivid color it appeared to be ra-
dioactive—Pernod, it was Pernod, how long had it been
since either of them had had a Pernod, how many years,
and could either of them remember?

Orange sadness is the sadness of anxiety and worry, it is the sadness of an orange balloon drifting over snow-capped mountains, the sadness of wild goats, the sadness of counting, as when one worries that another shipment of thoughts is about to enter the house, that a soufflé or Cessna will fall on the one day set aside to be unsad, it is the orange haze of a fox in the distance, it speaks the strange antlered language of phantoms and dead batteries, it is the sadness of all things left overnight in the oven and forgotten in the morning, and as such orange sadness becomes lost among us altogether, like its motive.

Yellow sadness is the surprise sadness. It is the sadness of naps and eggs, swan's down, sachet powder and moist towelettes. It is the citrus of sadness, and all things round and whole and dying like the sun possess this sadness, which is the sadness of the first place; it is the sadness of explosion and expansion, a blast furnace in Duluth that rises over the night skyline to fall reflected in the waters of Lake Superior, it is a superior joy and a superior sadness, that of revolving doors and turnstiles, it is the confusing sadness of the never-ending and the evanescent, it is the sadness of the jester in every pack of cards, the sadness of a poet pointing to a flower and saying *what is that* when what that is is a violet; yellow sadness is the ceiling fresco painted by Andrea Mantegna in the Castello di San Giorgio in Mantova, Italy, in the fifteenth century, wherein we look up to see we are being looked down upon, looked down upon in laughter and mirth, it is the sadness of that.

WILD FOREST BLOOD

Autumn upset the young fox—in his anger and fear he went home crying bitterly with a dirty face and sweet violets still clasped unconsciously in his scratchy little hand. In his den, which was not snug, he put the violets in a mustard jar on the table, and ate a poor supper of half a young rabbit that had been killed so long ago it could rightfully be called old. He could not stop crying. He wished he could turn the pages of autumn the way he turned the pages of a book, which was, when he had come to the bottom, to stare at the page and say *Turn!* Turn, turn, turn, he cried in his evening stupor, in his despair. But nothing happened. The leaves kept falling, their colors changing even as they fell, turning this way and that, little staple holes of light in every one. The wind repeated its autumn song. Fox was so fearful of that song he went to bed without a pillow, lodging it under his door to keep the song out. In bed, calmer, he began his nighttime reading, a mystery, one whose hero was a forensic analyst working for the police, poring over forged documents, analyzing their handwriting, the make of pen used, the age and origin of the ink. A self-taught expert, the hero could infer from ink alone that a signature was actually written on September 23, and not the 16th, the date the letter was signed. He used microscopes, chemicals, and spectrographs. In tonight's chapter he was investigating the paper itself, its smudges and folds, the date of manufacture, fiber composition, color, texture, gloss, finish, length, width, thickness, weight, markings, and imperfections. Fox stopped at a singular sentence, his eyes narrowing in concentration: *Even a little staple hole may be the beacon which will light up the truth.* He read it again. Tears came out of their ducts and rolled down the sides of his face. He took his pillow from under the door, placed it under his head on the bed, and listening to the autumn song he fell asleep, having made peace with autumn, and the wild forest blood in his veins.

INKY FLOURISH

More than one hundred years after his death, it was found that a manuscript by Charles Baudelaire, upon close inspection, bore not just an inky flourish between poems the way today's poet might type an asterisk between paragraphs, but that each inky flourish was in fact a floating swan, an aquanaut of gracefully curving neck and carefully upturned tail feathers. And it was following this discovery that a later manuscript was examined, and upon closer inspection was clearly seen to contain not just an inky flourish between poems but floating cellphones, the starship *Enterprise*, and American hot dogs in white buns with a caterpillar of yellow mustard slinking lengthwise along the dog. *But none of these things had yet been invented!* was the cry of the critic. Ah, Charles Baudelaire, the visionary visionary, who once said *Paris may change; my melancholy is fast*, you have crawled from the depths of antiquity, by means of your own inky flourish, straight into the heart of our present-day turmoil. What say you now, Charlie?

PERSONALIA

When I was young, a fortune-teller told me that an old woman who wanted to die had accidentally become lodged in my body. Slowly, over time, and taking great care in following esoteric instructions, including lavender baths and the ritual burial of keys in the backyard, I rid myself of her presence. Now I am an old woman who wants to die and lodged inside me is a young woman dying to live; I work on her.

OUTCAST

If a poet who lived two hundred or twenty-one hundred years ago, say Catullus or Coleridge, sprang to life to read a poem written last year, and in it the poet said *I was stoned*, either would assume the poet was an outcast, his body covered with tiny potholes from all the rocks the villagers had thrown at him. There would be surprise that the stoned poet was even still alive, just as the poet would be astonished Catullus or Coleridge had sprung to life again, and if the ancient went to the poet's house for a visit and was offered a cold beer, and the light inside the refrigerator popped on, the ancient would drop dead all over again from a heart attack induced by the shock of electrical incomprehension. Well, that's how it is—the stars reach me, I see their light. Someone once explained to me that the stars are dead, but when I look up I don't act as if suddenly hit, I act normally, as if I understood everything, and I never think of how cold it is two hundred or twenty-one hundred miles out, nor do I think for a moment Catullus or Coleridge ever did, which means I think there is no difference between us, even if I have led you to believe there is.

TOWARDS A
CAREFREE WORLD

Many of the most astonishing writers in the world had servants. It is doubtful they ever really washed the dishes. Which is too bad; I think they would have enjoyed washing the dishes, especially after dinner. Repetitive motion can take your mind off things. By *things* I mean the cares of this world. Repeated dish-washing can leave the hands chafed, but writers work also with their hands and often have, as a result of their work, a raised callus below the nail of the middle finger, formed by long contact and constant pressure between the flesh and the pen. It is doubtful Gustave Flaubert ever shoveled the snow in front of his home. It is interesting to imagine what his snow-shoveling style would have been, given the varying styles in which he wrote. Yet given the long hours of his working habits, we should not be surprised if his entire yard were emptied of snow. Shoveling takes your mind off things. Unless you are very troubled; in the case of the very troubled, no amount of shoveling snow or washing dishes will remove one's cares from the mind. Servants who did not own the land where the snow fell upon the house where the dishes were kept might have been very troubled. Money, illness, death, relations with others, including relatives: these are chief among our human woes; writers choose their subjects from among them. Long hours spent working on a novel, a story, a play, or a poem might also take one's mind off things. It seems strange, but possible, to use troubles to take your mind off of them. Perhaps the writer is a servant in his own way. I do not know who hires such servants, but the world seems full of them, ready for hire. If each household hired a writer-servant to sit and concentrate on the human troubles we each must bear, every household might be free from care. Yet it is hardly practical to hire a writer to sit in one's house all day, an extra room would be needed, and an extra servant hired to keep the children and animals quiet, so as not to disturb the writer, who, like all living things, must also be fed. And so the world has hit upon an ingenious plan involving books, which are relatively easy to bring into the house, take up but a small space, and never need to be fed: inside each book sits a servant with a callus on his finger, the author, who has concentrated on the cares of this world so that our minds may be free of them, as anyone knows who has ever sat for hours reading a book—the world seems far, far away, one forgets the time, one is surprised to look up and discover her own feet, which seem far, far away at that moment, or a potted plant on the other side of the room—where did it come from, how long has it been there? If a household employs servants to wash the dishes, shovel the snow, and water the plants, the reader is left doubly, even triply, carefree. But how odd, how very odd, that so many households containing a great many books, or a great many other things in any combination, are not exempt from care. In fact a great many cares find lodging there. It is deeply troubling to think that servants of any kind cannot fulfill their tasks to the extent we are left completely carefree. The servants need to work harder, or we need to have more of them; it is hard to know what to do, yet it seems obvious that something need be done.

SELF-CRITICISM

In a typical poem by myself, a woman is sitting alone doing absolutely nothing. She notices a fly crawling across the table and strikes up a conversation with him. Something terribly dramatic happens, and the poem ends. This happens day after day, as many days as there are poems in a book, leaving her exhausted.

White sadness is the sadness of teeth, bones, fingernails, and stars, yes, but it is also the sadness of cereal, shower caps, and literary foam, it is the sadness of Aunt Jenny's white hair covering her body like a sheet, down to her toes, as she lay on the sickbed, terrifying the children who were brought in one by one to say goodbye. It is the sadness of radio waves traveling through space forever, it is the voice of John Lennon being interviewed, his voice growing weaker and weaker as the waves pass eternally through a succession of galaxies, not quite there, but still . . .

Brown sadness is the simple sadness. It is the sadness of huge, upright stones. That is all. It is simple. Huge, upright stones surround the other sadnesses, and protect them. A circle of huge, upright stones—who would have thought it?

THEY WERE WRONG

They say a picture is worth a thousand words, but I never believed them. They say all writing is an argument with the world, but I've never met them, and besides, I no longer live in this or any other world. Where do I live? you ask. I live in a fog, a haze, and the drowsy fumes of daylight make me want to sleep. To sleep, you will recall, is to leave this world, and as soon as you wake you must jump on a carousel if you want to catch back up. It makes me yawn, it makes me put ketchup on my eggs which makes a bloody mess. Now I'm tired again and this is serious business. I need some flowers. A little trip, no more than twenty minutes, to the grocery store and back, that will do the wake-up trick. A big fresh bouquet of flowers lolling around in a vase on the table and I'll be fine. Sometimes just looking at something can produce a powerful shock of adrenaline. But you mustn't go further than that—you mustn't bend down to smell the flowers, that would be disastrous, their fumes would bring too much peace: so much peace coursing through your body would cause another yawn. Now I am in my car, I am on my way to the flowers, and I find traffic peaceful when it is backed up at a stoplight. Just sitting here—I'm in the driver's seat of course—with a car in front of me and a car behind me, is profoundly *nice*. It feels right, it feels like everything is exactly the way it is supposed to be, as if everything that ever happened from the beginning of all events, time chief among them, has led to this very line of cars at this very red light; the death of dinosaurs, men and women living in caves, the weaving of cloaks, the whole Middle Ages, the cultivation of maize, the suckling of a little boy who will grow up and die in the wrestling ring—all these things led to this moment, a moment of bluish exhaust rising from the tailpipes of cars as peacefully as smoke from the pipe of an old sailor. Now the light has changed and this historical moment of peace is gone, we are moving forward, I am moving forward towards my flowers and another is moving forward towards his can of soup, still another moving towards, who knows, a sooner death than any of the other customers. In the parking lot I want to sleep but open the door in a great effort to meet the air. Soon I am in the mart itself, I am in the ninth aisle, I am not pushing a cart or anything else, I have never had a baby, I am free and virginal, walking down the aisle on my own two dangling legs, and at the end of the aisle is a garden of leaves and blossoms, I am in the garden, there are plants and flowers, everything is green and alive and growing and there are masses of color to choose from, red, yellow, orange, white, purple, a man is buying flowers for his wife, pink roses wrapped in cellophane—could anything be more idyllic, less argumentative, than that? Yet I want to speak. *Stop*, I say, as the man bends down over his flowers, flowers that will in time move on and belong to his wife, *please don't smell the roses*—but it is too late, he has done it—and now I can smell them, too—the air is saturated with sacred attar—and I, who was so close to being energized, who came all this way from the beginning of time, want nothing now but to fall asleep, to lie down on the floor at the end of the ninth aisle, among the houseplants, and sleep the sleep of ages, having spoken to a man who ignored my sage advice, and now looks as tired of the world as I am.

THE GIFT

The day the living room flooded I had not left the apart-
ment in five days, everything was spotlessly clean, I had
no work to do except writing my thoughts in a journal,
the thought of which filled me with terror and boredom.
That fateful and final morning I was in bed reading, un-
able to concentrate because of what I had done the day
before. The day before I had ordered by telephone a large
gift box of glacé apricots from Australia. The catalogue,
South Sea Gifts, showed the fruit in a handsome wooden
crate, lined with gold foil. They cost $86.20 and I had
them sent to myself with a gift card that said *from Mary
to Mary*. I was uneasy because I now had no money to buy
groceries with and it would be some time before the apri-
cots arrived, even though I had them sent express, which
cost more. I looked forward to their arrival but at the same
time they would, when they arrived, only remind me of
my stupidity and terrible guilt. My guilt was tremendous.
To have used the last of my money sending myself a gift
of glacé apricots! And the gold foil—that had cost more,
too. The cheaper "home boxes" had more apricots in

them, but were without gold foil. The gold foil looked so nice, shining beside the golden apricots. Of course I had been looking at a photograph, and I worried that the picture was somehow "touched up," because I once met a food stylist whose job it was to make photographs of food look better than the food itself; she used glycerin and starch and hairspray to make things luscious and shining, crisp, fresh, mouthwatering in a tantalizing way. I didn't want to open the box and be disappointed. I also thought of ordering a circle of white cotton mosquito netting, but came to my senses. At least I could eat the apricots. What would I do with mosquito netting? I just like the way it looks—you can drape it over anything and the draped thing becomes soft and mysterious. I read an article once about a woman who was an intensely intellectual Buddhist and she wanted to make her house as empty and white as possible, but she owned thousands of books, which dragged the energy of the space down, so she simply made vertical pillars of her books and draped them with mosquito netting and got the effect she was after—the effect of owning nothing, wanting nothing, living in a windswept environment of peace. All my extravagant mail-ordering—it had me feeling uneasy. I felt vapid and shallow and guilty, I loved my books and just the sight of them strewn around on low-lying tables and lined up on windowsills and stacked on the floor—along with catalogues and unopened bills—had always made me feel happy in a teeming, chaotic way, and gave me the feeling my life was full and interesting, that I was a serious and charming person. I also worried about the people who answered the phone for the catalogue companies—did they have enough to eat? Did they ever steal a glacé apricot or two? I knew they had work, they had to answer phone calls, they had to calm the caller down and answer all her questions, they had to explain the difference between a "gift box" and a "home box." I could see them in a cavernous room, sitting in makeshift booths with earphones on. For some reason I draped them all with mosquito netting, I mean each one individually wore a cocoon of soft white gauze. It muffled their voices while they spoke to the customer, she had to ask them to repeat what they just said, so an endless loop of repetition began to bubble up from the cocoons. That's how I pictured it. It was then that I heard the water in the living room, bubbling up from some mysterious source. I got out of bed to investigate and as soon as I entered the hall I saw a pool of brown water advancing toward my feet. I had forgotten to put on slippers, I was standing in my bare feet, and the brown water came up over my ankles. I waded forward toward the living room. The sofa was covered with mud and pieces of debris—sticks and clumps of leaves, the black gunk that closes off a rain gutter. There was a high-water mark on the television screen, a wavy white salt horizon that crossed the black glass. My books, too, were covered with the wavy lines of loose, disintegrating matter—detritus, I believe it is called. Some piglets were scavenging the place, eating the stuffing out of a chair in the corner, a chair I always read in. Why did I decide to read in bed that morning? I don't know. It was highly unusual. Everything was waterlogged, the legs of the table looked soft, like they were made of oatmeal, and a mass riot of spiders swarmed on top of my table, the way I've seen ants swarm under my welcome mat outside. The flood had obviously subsided. It must have happened during the night when I was sleeping. I thought for a moment that there was a bloated corpse on the floor, but it was just a sack of rotten potatoes that had floated out from under the sink and was stranded in the stagnant water, a gelatinous mass, puffed up and green. I'm ashamed to say my first thought was that I could not possibly clean up this mess by myself; I needed help. And what about those piglets in the corner, devouring my chair? Where did they come from? The place stank. It smelled worse than a sewer. It smelled like a petri dish of primordial ooze and whoever I called for help would have to cordon off more than my living room: the entire building and the block it sat upon would have to be cordoned off too. And in this way another day of potential reverie had been broken in two, utterly destroyed by my desire for an apricot, a single indiscretion for which my habitat had become a village of sticks on the banks of a rising river, where trade winds blew and the rains came and mosquitoes bred; and where mosquitoes breed, one will be needing some netting.

THE INVASIVE THING

In the beginning I suppose there were crumbs, a little something that fell from the crack of the mouth, a chip off the hunk. These crumbs on my kitchen counter look like a scattering of stars, though they are not much bigger than grains of salt, and made of toast, burnt bread. There are those (I have seem them too) who do not notice such things as crumbs, and if pointed out to them, consider crumbs as natural as a tree and as unremarkable as anything that goes unnoticed. But a tree! A tree is a gigantic plant, the most gigantic plant on the planet. Nothing is larger than a tree, unless it is man-made or made of rock. In this trees are remarkable, beyond any individual characteristics each may possess (I once saw a picture of a cactus with cancer which was beautiful in its branching mutations). Most things, I have noticed, have the right to exist and stay as they are. My hand, for example, has a mind of its own. I cannot say who sees the crumbs first, my eyes or my hands, but my fingers begin to crouch in preparation for what happens next: I move the crumbs with my crouching hand over the edge of the counter, where they fall into the palm of my other hand, which began to open as soon as the other began to crouch. I do not know which is the Invasive Thing, my hands or the crumbs, for the invasive plant grows wild and free, cancer cells multiply with joy and a mind of their own, and the planets inhabit what was once an infinite emptiness we do our own small part in filling, not only by existing (even if unnoticed) but also by all our minute and repetitive actions, such as cleaning crumbs from a countertop, which is as empty now as it ever was, and the crumbs sealed in the total darkness of a black plastic bag that sooner or later I will carry out.

THE SUBLIME

Had no warning of what to expect, no sign of sharp curves. Hadn't gone far when I came to hairpin turns every few hundred feet—on both sides of me deep canyons with only a few scrimpy bushes between me and the Abyss. My hair stood on end. The road was narrow then narrower, turning this way and that as I climbed, hunched over the steering wheel. Could see from the corner of my eye that there was an incredible view, but couldn't look.

A STRANGE THING

Maybe I read this, or dreamt it, for my mind wanders as I age, but I have always believed Odysseus, when he heard the sirens, was hearing the *Odyssey* being sung, and in fear of being seduced by his own story he had himself bound. And he was in even greater fear of hearing the end, for he could not bear the possibility he might become someone other than who he was now, a war hero of great courage and unexcelled strategy, trembling against the cords at his own mast. Or he might become an even greater man, one without a single fear in the world, one who would balk at a man having to tie himself up in fear of anything, and then it would be revealed that the man he was now was actually a coward. Either way, he felt doomed as he sailed past his own story. He sailed past the island, he sailed past the sirens just as they were coming to the end, and once out of earshot he did a strange thing, of which there is no record, the story having ended in some faraway sound that was no more distinguishable than an eyedropper of sweetness in the vast and salty sea.

ACKNOWLEDGMENTS

I am grateful to the editors of the following magazines and journals, where many of these pieces first appeared or were reprinted: *The Best American Poetry, Diagram, Ecotone, The Fabulist, Granta, Harper's, The Hoot & Hare Review, Kenyon Review, The Lumberyard, MAKE: A Literary Magazine, Matrix, Music & Literature, Paris Review, Storyscape, Tin House,* and *Unstuck.*

*

Author's note: In each of the color pieces, if you substitute the word *happiness* for the word *sadness*, nothing changes.